"Poet Franco Pagnucci brings his passion for nature and the beauty of the North Carolina coast to life in his new book, *Intracoastal*. Readers are taken on a journey through the seasons, experiencing the calls of sandpipers and the beauty of the coastal waters. With nine poetry books to his credit, you don't want to miss this newest addition."

—Stephanie Edwards, Librarian, Onslow County Public Library – Swansboro Branch

"The quiet, emotional pull in Pagnucci's lovely poetry speaks to both change and continuity. In *Intracoastal*, the speaker's move from North to South, the loss of friends, and the growing up of children is counterposed to the everyday presence of crabs, osprey, herons, and gulls, which anchors him to the natural world. There is gratitude, here, too—not only for the beauty of the salt marsh— but for life, love, and human connection. This gorgeous book takes my breath away."

—Laura C. Wendorff, Professor Emeritus in English, UW – Platteville

"Pagnucci is a master of the written word, and his most recent book of poems will not disappoint! Locals and visitors alike will be transported to the beautiful North Carolina coast by Pagnucci's latest work. His vivid descriptions allow the reader to almost feel the warm ocean breezes, hear the crashing waves and catch sight of shiny black dolphins diving in the surf. His love of the ocean and local salt marsh, interwoven with his long-lasting passion for his wife, shine through in this latest book. Bravo!"

—Stacy H. Nelson, BS, RAC - US

"Pagnucci has spun the poetic yarn once more to produce a new collection of verse in *Intracoastal*. With inspiration drawn mostly from his daily walks with wife on trails, marshlands, and beaches of Eastern North Carolina, Pagnucci has crafted a fresh angle that blends the nuances of nature with the heartstrings of family and the human experience. As always, Pagnucci's writing is movingly poignant, conveying much between the lines of few words, allowing one's imagination to roam. Subtle shifts in thought give way to the unexpected hidden love story of the pair, now in later years, with a nod to romance and a hint of sensuality ('Black Magnolias,' 'Walkers in the Marsh.') Transcendent and endearing, the tone of these poems takes a sweep at past, present, and even the future cycle of human relationship co-existence with nature."

—Paula Patselas, President, Friends of Swansboro Library

"*Intracoastal*, Franco Pagnucci's ninth book, follows a couple's journey from the woods of northwestern Wisconsin to the coastal plain of North Carolina. Their relocation and education is the love story at the heart of this lovely book. And though the new world they encounter is sometimes as hostile as a hurricane, ultimately they find equilibrium with the help of nature: 'the tricolored heron' waiting 'on a post of a bridge rail' stays still while the walkers get close enough to 'close the gap,' letting 'warmth' spread 'outward,' as if the heron knows. This one is a must read."

—William K. Spofford, Emeritus Professor UW-Platteville

INTRACOASTAL

Franco Pagnucci

WATER'S EDGE PRESS
TUCSON, AZ

For Susan and our family
and all our friends near and far.

This collection of poems is a human-made work of imagination. No part of this book may be reproduced, distributed, or transmitted in any form or by any means without written permission of the publisher, except in the case of brief quotations used in a review of the book.

NO AI TRAINING: Without in any way limiting the author's [and publisher's] exclusive rights under copyright, any use of this publication to "train" generative artificial intelligence (AI) technologies to generate text is expressly prohibited. The author reserves all rights to license uses of this work for generative AI training and development of machine learning language models.

Intracoastal © Franco Pagnucci, 2025
All rights reserved.

ISBN: 978-1-952526-30-5

Published in the United States

Water's Edge Press
Tucson, Arizona

Credits:
Cover and author photos by Susan Pagnucci
Original artwork by Franco Pagnucci
Cover and book design by Water's Edge Press

The Call

The Call 1
Daughters 2
When You Know the Way Back 4
Winter Calm 5
End of January 6
Our Days Now 7
We'd Heard Peepers 8
One-legged Sandpiper 9
Spartina 10
Emerald Isle 11
February Fog 12
Then 13
In the Tidal Zone 14
We Went to the Ocean 15
You Pucker Your Mouth to Blow in a Conch ... 16
After the Walk 17

The Pond

The Pond 21
After *Florence* 22
Four Osprey Nests 23
Ground Wind 24
Heading Back 25
Late December Sky 26
The Talker 27
The Atlantic Was Calm 28
On the Beach New Year's Day 29
Snowbirds 30
January Saturday, 2019 32
Moon Jellyfish 33

We Go to the Salt Marsh 34
When the New Moon Was Full 35
For the Great Egret 36
Two Seagulls 37
Puffer Fish 38
Claude Monet 39
Warm Shivers Rose Up Our Legs 40
After the Rain 41
An Aviary 42
Loblolly Pines, Live Oaks, Red Cedars 43
From a Bridge 44
Black Magnolias 45
Snakes 46
Every Day We Go to the Salt Marsh 47
Five-tab Shingles 48
Walkers in the Marsh 49
It Had Been a Good Winter 50

Two Worlds

Wild Grape Vines 53
Two Worlds 54
Low or High Tide 55
The Preacher 56
Winter in the Marsh I 58
Winter in the Marsh II 59
Where the Croatan Touches the Marsh 60
When the Tide Was Out 61
Late January, 2020 62
Frost 63
The Last Walker 64
Canopy of Trees 65
Two Willets 66
Easy to Love 67

Homecoming 68
The Neighbor's Holly 69
When the Heron Paced 70
When Spring Came 71
The Pull 72
Ash Wednesday Night 73
On the Boat Landing Dock 74
I Was the Salt Marsh 75
Morning Concert 76
Late March 77
The Willets' Way 78
Dubling Creek 79
All That Spring 80
Two Looking at Two 81
When You Stopped 82
We Met As in a Dream 83
Sunday Morning 84
After Islander Beach Opened Again 85

"no hay camino, se hace al andar."
"there is no path, the path is made by walking."

—Antonio Machado

THE CALL

The Call

for Sylvia & Deb

Leaves were falling colors—
too soon
in too chill an air.

In spring, robins
had crowded our places.
Now robins and more robins
rushing through.

And we awoke
with dull aches in a hip,
a shoulder, under a knee cap.

After two days of rain
only the oaks had leaves,
curled and brown.
At dawn the tearing away

from neighbors, lakes, trees—
a cold-potato knot in the chest.
Then the long journey south.

Daughters

for Bill & daughter Lee Ann

That year's offspring hung around,
sitting on her favorite branch
four feet above the nest,
calling out—

So sad a cry,
Kathy our young neighbor said.
*Makes you feel sad. And every day
that sad cry!*

It was autumn
in the north lake country.
Sunny. Cool that day.
The rains for a while were gone.
Full fall colors falling fast.

Then, in early October
the immature hadn't come back.
All night. In the morning one of the adults
sat silent above the nest. No calls out.
Even as I came up from the house
and started piling brush to haul away.

This was a fall ending. Since early July
we had waited for the eaglet to fly,
but everything that year was late.

When our son dropped his daughter off for college,
he tried to help set up her bunk until she said
she was going to get her books.

That was the sign, he said
I realized I wasn't needed anymore.
The two-hour drive home was silent.

Time goes so fast.
The little things are what we remember.
Pushes on the park swings. Quiet talks before school.
The house, then, he said, *was suddenly very quiet.*

My new friend Schmelzer, a professional psychologist,
when he told me about his daughter's
approaching marriage, choked.
Couldn't say where she was moving,
touched me on the shoulder so I'd understand.
Leaving home is a fall ending.

That early October day, the bald eagle sitting,
all morning sitting so silent,
made me miss my daughter
building their place fifteen-hundred miles away
along the salt flats of North Carolina.

When You Know the Way Back

The wooden shelter sits at the top of the steps
that rise between protected sand dunes.

You can stop and look back
from where you have come—
the walk, the climb, the journey.

The path to the horizon is there on the Atlantic.
The light sparkles even on gray afternoons.

Winter Calm

Walking west as usual,
we found
even the soft wash of the sea
too loud
for our litany of worries.

End of January

We sat on the white bench swing swinging

and saw two, then three dolphins
break the flat surface of the water and swim west,
headed home in the sea.

Tides rose and fell back.

Every day we walked coast or salt marsh,
watching the changing light
and looking for our place.

Our Days Now

Walking Emerald Isle Beach,
you are diminished
under the loud tow of the ocean.

Heavens and earths come
and vanish in each tumble and crash.

Forgiveness gurgles
up your throat. What can
we do about anything?

Tweets unnerve us, and training explosions
from the Marine camp rattle our windows

day and night.
A heart can feel off center.
Even open-eyed we could be

in Bagdad or Kabul
or on any street in the white fire's rage.

We'd Heard Peepers

It wasn't April, and we were far,
far from Wisconsin,
but roadside swales swelled
after days of heavy downpours, lingering.
Dusks flirted with light that held the day's warmth close.

What could peepers do? They sang.
They sang and sang into the fallen dark.
And half the night we heard them.

One-legged Sandpiper

Still he is there
with the rest, working—
cool wind blowing.
He's learned to make do
one-legged. A cold surf
retreats, and he pecks

tiny crabs that bury themselves
in wet sand—this seasoned
picker. His family waits
in a one room, windowless
place with hope and a song.

Spartina

Tall and reed-like, it grows.
By March the inlet banks are lush.
Early April its tall, hairy leaves hide
tall egrets standing out of wind
on muddy inlet banks, fishing.

And it spends its days
sweating salts and storing oxygen
for neighbors,
in her green, the bright spots—
thin-necked, great white egrets,
great blue herons.
Even ospreys from tall
shore pines will come down
for the fish in her lap.

And we who pass and stop often
along bridge rails
to marvel at fiddler crabs
on the mud flats
hardly see the emerald sea of cord grass.

Emerald Isle

We walk west along the strand
and come back.
The sea washes in from the east
and backs out.

Sometimes we turn toward each other
and smile.
We know this world is not ours.

February Fog

That day when the fog
sat heavy on the sea
and our world all but disappeared,
two doves came down along the louvered strand.

The deep roaring closer,
he followed at her heels
but two steps above her,
bobbing his male head in that knowing way.

On the inside he was us,
stomach muscles twitching,
heart saying, *Admit it.*
Admit it! You're lost.

Then

That fiddler crab that crossed our path the morning
the tide was out far and the sun heavy on the salt marsh flats,
you couldn't miss the green and pollen—
the yellow glow of his giant claw paraded above his muddied head.

In the Tidal Zone

Scurrying the surf's edge three sanderlings
pecking for tiny crabs burrowing.
To keep their feet dry they'll have to run,
leaning into an inclining strand.

So why do we chase them,
if not to make them sprint and hurl themselves
into the air and screech out their alarm,
Kip! Kip! Kip! Awayeeee? Awayeeee?

We Went to the Ocean

Waves were ducking.
The few ring-billed gulls
sat on their bellies
legs tucked under breast feathers.

A cold northwest wind
raised waves of sand
and made walls burying the gulls.

It sandblasted us
and shoved us back
to say we didn't belong.

The gulls squinted
and closed their eyes.
The waves ducked
and walked away.

You Pucker Your Mouth to Blow in a Conch

We always have to imagine
the whole from the pieces
we find as the tide
washes out.
But you're never sure.
A twist, a curve,
an envisioned
shading
blush of amber
might be all wrong.
You're left with parts
of perfection only imagined
while the tide rushes in again.

After the Walk

When you left the strand
and reentered
the whoosh of traffic,
morning gripes honking around you,
still, you could feel
fine sand grains
between your toes,
in your ears the wash of the sea.

THE POND

The Pond

for Kathy

It's a gathering place.
Croatan Indians must have stopped
for the cool waters of the spring.
We late ones were mainly searching
for the sun for our last years.

Here we watch younger, more nomadic
neighbors. Small gray squirrels live here,
thrive, and multiply on the hard hickory nut.
Herons and egrets sometimes stop to fish.

After *Florence*

A neighbor sand-bagged
the burst pond dam
and for a while
saved the three old, titan carp.

Then the great blue heron
came daily,
walked the length and flew back,
walked the length again

as if he was bent
under heavy thought
like a silent monk in prayer,
praying for us all.

When a fish flashed
in his gulping bill,
no scales flew,
his world measurable and calm.

Four Osprey Nests

Florence blew them down,
and the salt flats were empty.
The fiddler crabs were gone.
Maybe, they too, had been uprooted
and displaced by the storm.
The smallest among us,
then, needed our deep concern.

Ground Wind

It flattened the ocean
and made waves duck.
So they lowered their shoulders
backing away.
Offshore some gulls faced inland
hunkering their bellies
into sand walling around them.
Others stood on one foot,
maybe a bad leg tucked up,
a restless injury
kept close and still.

Heading Back

Heading back
over waves of dry sand,
you hear the grains sing underfoot.

The ocean grows distant.
The tide going out leaves a whisper inside us

seeping between fissures
and crevices. It spreads through dry places.
The sparkle of water rushes the edge of the horizon.
In the gray afternoon, I wait for you.

Late December Sky

Behind your shoulders the Highway 24
bridge frames the White Oak River.

A man in a red flannel shirt
zooms down river thinking friction-
speed through wind makes him less cold.

We split a Granwich of a filet of cheap,
farmed Asian fish some believe tastes like grouper.
Flocks of slate-gray pigeons bank left over the river
as if they are swerving over the Tiber.

The Talker

Blustery Saturday, 8:30 a.m.,
wind at twenty-three knots.

All day Friday it rained,
next day the salt marsh rich
in rainwater even over some trails.

The Navy Vet and only walker, then,
was leaving but needed to talk.
In the boat landing parking lot, we listened.

Assumptions in the news reminded him of Cincinnati
where wind on a Bluff off the Ohio and maybe—
a condor, some said, *snatched a child.*

His smile, wry. Aware of the cold
and our urge to move,

he said, *I did the trails first.*
If you do, you'll hit the bridges
with the wind at your back.

The Atlantic Was Calm

calmer than we'd seen in a month.

The strand lay littered with tiny shells, homes of lost creatures.
That night a full moon, a blood moon would rise
closer than usual to earth—the full pull.

We'd see it and want to rush out too. Naked,
we'd scatter our fondest memories, attachments, our fears.

On the Beach New Year's Day

Worries dropped
and night stuffiness.
Your bag heavy with shells
and shards of lost creatures
clinking against each other
awakened voices.
How lucky to have been together
walking west with the new day.

Snowbirds

1

Late December-January days when a chill wind blew
and we were happy we'd packed light winter coats
and the tide was out,
we considered our blessings—
being able to walk
and walk well and together along the strand.
You lingered searching, smiling
even with half a sliver of sand dollar.

2.

There were days when I sometimes missed snowbanks
we'd left along our road through Wisconsin woods
where pines whispered in our dreams.

3

On the long journey down, we'd passed RVers
streaming south like snow flurries on the wind.
We tried to recognize them and make up stories.
There are White Cities, RV towns (Quartzsite, Arizona).
Texas calls snowbirds Winter Texans.
Florida swells with them.
We'd seen pictures of Pinecraft, Florida (origin, 1925),
Las Vegas to the Amish on their three-wheeled bikes.
Even the summery air above them was all smiles.

4

The retired fella at the back of the library book group
got a cheer when he said, *Cape Carteret,*
where I live now,
with all the birds, the salt marsh, the ocean,
our community of neighbors,
the thoughtful care for land and water....
It is, he said, *how I imagine heaven.*

5

Walking the beach those days
when the tide went far, far
and I missed the ice-encrusted snow
louvered toward our lakeshore,
I wondered if those men and women
on their trikes in Pinecraft
and whose smiles are hidden behind
the photo ever missed their horses.

6

Horses in graying November fields
in Iowa, Wisconsin, Ohio, Pennsylvania.
Horses standing close together,
broad backs and broad buttocks to the wind.

January Saturday, 2019

We head west.
Soft waves.
Morning light warms our backsides.

A line of pelicans
comes toward us, skims the flat waves,
where yesterday we watched them stop,
fold wings like closing umbrellas,
and dive into white caps.

Today we could be watched.
Walking back east into the sun,
where two, then three dolphins cut the sea surface,
we stop, closer than waking lovers.

Moon Jellyfish

Clouds covered the big moon.
The night, the old narrow Highway turned deep-ocean black.
Suddenly a black cotton picker the size of a two-story house
took most of the two lanes.
You ricocheted us off the double-wheeled
six-foot-high tires to a stop.
Windows shattered. The Traverse totaled.
We were saved inside,
pillowed by airbags as in a coffin.

In the morning, dazed,
we walked the shore west along a stretch of sand
where jellyfish lay like fallen leaves curled and drying,
the dark night, the storm, the high tide now far, far.
Then we saw the jellyfish, blueish, translucent, an inverted saucer,
a pulsing moon with a rim like the edge of an umbrella.

Out of the blackness of storms, it was here.
It could make us remember the dark.
Still, it was beautiful. Still we felt the wash of the sea fill us.

We Go to the Salt Marsh

Sunday. Mid-morning.
Marine artillery from Camp Lejeune
rattles our world like far off thunder.
All day. A chopper cuts east to west.

At the back of Swansboro,
behind the white water tower,
shades of low dark clouds in the distance.

Here the sun warms swaying marsh grass.
In a far inlet of tidewater, a flash of silver
in a white egret's bill. You lead. Happily,

I follow over the curving bridge-trail.
A runner passes, running on tiptoes.
In yellow jersey, she could be a sulfur
butterfly. She slips through like a whisper.

When the New Moon Was Full

The all-high tide flooded the marsh again
and spread a coating of pollen over the salt flats.

Yellow dust gave itself to the windy air.

Along a footpath bridge railing,
we stopped to encircle initials in the yellow powder.
It could have been that early spring in Illinois

when we first met and our two wills linked.

Springs have had a way with us, and here we were
new in a new place blessed to be walking together.

For the Great Egret

It appeared, a white-feathered fossil
entangled atop a twisted pile of uprooted
trees and broken, browning branches.

Maybe a flicker of thought on a rising turn
distracted the left eye looking too long
across the salt marsh. Imagine

how in a sudden twinge of knee pain
your memory snaps the head and feet back
to the path where a gnarl of root snaking out

catches you. So. That bird's slender
feet and legs might have drooped
and dragged an instant and snagged

a loop out of a tangle of brush. There
the great hook of the universe caught the bird
mid-flight. He came down, then, on a moldering

pile the hurricane driven sea left at the edge
of the elevated footpath. And he lay
neck broken, spread wings bleaching in the sun.

Two Seagulls

They stood alone in that stretch,
a hundred feet apart, backs to the ocean,
their feathers lifted and dropped by a cold wind.

Rivulets from the high tide ran back to the sea.
Sand underfoot was soupy.
Still side by side we walked the edge, feeling lucky.
Waves from far out crashed. Lonely logs of salty foam rolled in.

Puffer Fish

You would have said
the three were dead,
yet the one closest
to us seemed to breathe.

The back rose and fell.

When a wave came in
and rocked that fish
toward us and back,
maybe it shivered and awoke.

A second wave heavy with grit
and a blanket of sand gathered it to itself.

Claude Monet

Outside St. Mildred's Church. February.
Orange sinking below a roll of black clouds.
A chill wind off the Atlantic from the north.

Hear the peepers? I said to the woman
bent over her cane
in the last of the light.

She stopped and swiveled her head my way.
*Peepers are tree frogs that come
down to mate*, I said. *The first sign of spring.*

Thanks for sharing, she said.
I needed that. She smiled and swiveled her head
back, and we walked under a tinge of orange to our cars.

Warm Shivers Rose Up Our Legs

and waves sometimes nipped
at our heels and made us leap.

And then there were dolphins—
black backs arching out of the waves,
black-tipped dorsal fins
cutting through water and air.

And everybody along the beach stopped and stood still.

After the Rain

The few feathers caught
between uprooted trees
and fractured browning branches
where the great egret crashed
and died had disappeared,

and we who had seen the bird
and remembered
couldn't point to the place for sure.

Today a mourning dove
called out of a nearby tree
greening in the morning sun.
Another answered and came closer.

An Aviary

From the dead tops of high pines, they whistled
and dove, three, four, five ospreys
in and out of each other's loops.

They flew up, banking over the edge
of the Croatan Forest and came back around.
We stopped on a footpath bridge to look up,

squinting into a sky of bright clouds.
Late arrivals, under a spell of forgetful
sleep, we sometimes stood dazed.

Still we were amazed by the small, quiet place,
coming back, the *Great September Storm* forgotten,
uprooted trees and fractured branches holding new greens.

Loblolly Pines, Live Oaks, Red Cedars

Florence forced them down
on hands and knees. Many
entangled in themselves with upturned
roots and splintered branches were dying.

Still others hung back
and then leaned into the trails.
They shielded us from the clamors.
Their uplift lifted us. Our insides grew light,

our arms and shoulders reaching
for the sky, encouraging treetops up.

From a Bridge

for Natalia

You may see fiddlers
scurrying along the mud flats of the salt marsh
when the tide is out.

On a hot morning
watch them stuff their little mouths with the short claw,
the large one above their shoulders
greeting the day like middle schoolers carrying cellos in black cases.

Close your eyes in the warm silence
and some bright girl might ply her bow
across the strings—Bach to Yo-Yo Ma, half a prelude of Suite # 1
out of her small hands—
this precious world spinning its daily song under our feet.

Black Magnolias

The sun had lifted the early chill
that riffled our neck hairs. Four ospreys
circled the spring air, their whistles

above the loblolly pines circled
our heads, enchanting our eyes.
Reaching for clouds, we grew dizzy

and stopped on a bridge path to look down
at a bed of black oysters coated
in wet black mud—black magnolias!

We began to shed our extra
layers. I thought of undressing.
Ahead, you carried your own thoughts.

Snakes

The woman coming out the trail on the far side
of the marsh closest to the Croatan Forest
said it was black and big and stretched across

the entire path. *It made her cry,* said the guy
walking with her. The other woman with them
shook her head up and down. Up and down.

The Navy Vet who'd never seen a death in the salt
marsh in twenty-five years of walking there
rose from a bench and came over to show

a photo of what he'd seen on a path that morning.
He'd been waiting to talk about Good and Evil
in the world these days. This one had yellow
markings on black. *There are vipers*, he said.

The cottonmouth. Earlier he'd warned us
about poison ivy hanging from trees into trails.
I had no glasses to look closely but believed he knew snakes.

Every Day We Go to the Salt Marsh

Gravel paths skirt the edge in and out
of the Croatan Forest. Metal-slatted,
raised footpath bridges wind over
estuaries of Dubling Creek and marsh

rivulets. It's no paradise. Plants, animals
must swallow constant change from low and high
tides. The last hurricane's blowdowns litter
the woods. Dry combustible smells of crushed

trees and branches browning engulf you
when wind is still. Today deerflies suddenly
at every bend urge you to turn back. There
are places you have to duck poison ivy

hanging over paths, places the rotten-
eggs-muck smell makes you hold your breath and want
to run. Still in places a skyward fragrance
of pines, cedars, and greens raise our hands and arms.

Five-tab Shingles

Except for an occasional repair
most roofs wrecked by *Florence*
had been replaced,
and the Mexican crews were gone
to other neighborhoods. That morning

before dawn the barred owl nailed
her music like a five-tab shingle
across our waking: *hoot, hoot-hoot, hoot, hoot.*

I turned toward you, then, wondering
if you'd heard and were awake
and were thinking how our world was
coming back and if you, too, wanted to hold
us and it safe between us for the while.

Walkers in the Marsh

1

When their dogs
run with too long a leash,
you might see my love
cross her arms over her chest
and knot herself.

It will take half a trail loop
and a pass over a salt marsh bridge path
before her blue eyes loosen
and sparkle in the morning light.

2

I have stopped to sweep away
dog poop someone didn't own up to.

Mostly I am content walking,
watching my shifting attitudes.
I see the back of her ankles, so thin
I'd like to run a thumb and index finger
along the smoothness of their dips.

It Had Been a Good Winter

for Giada

Mostly. Again, we were leaving.
Now the younger neighbors and their children.
Nathan, the youngest, charged a lawn full of lazy robins.
They scattered in air like wispy clouds.

We drove west, Highway 58 toward the state's interior,
away from Emerald Isle, the ocean, the healing,
greening Salt Marsh, turned northeast on 95 to Virginia,
Maryland, and mountains of Pennsylvania.

Susan's right eye would continue clearing,
my jaw pain, easing, maybe in Wisconsin.
The ten-year-old granddaughter, "Button," for texting,
got taller and picked her band instrument.
Her wrist and arm were mending.

She'd learned to accept pain,
the loss of soccer season, cello lessons,
and to taste the humility of sideline watching—
like being too young again.
We'd miss her sleepovers and Sunday morning waffles.

TWO WORLDS

Wild Grape Vines

turn golden with trumpet vines.
The chains loop Croatan Forest to the marsh on the way to the sea.

Passing birds—
great white egrets, great blue herons, white ibis hang close.
We begin to count them in our mornings.
They feed us, loop us to their world as
we walk salt marsh and seashore

to the end of days ...
Then, we'll carry their memory like dying cord grasses
that sift sea salts from water and store oxygen
for plants and creatures.

Two Worlds

The tricolored heron
waited on a post of a bridge rail.
It turned as you stepped close
enough to close the gap
between your worlds.

I thought you could
have reached out then, caressed
a wing. She must have felt
the loop close and trusted

and stayed still in that warmth
spreading outward,
though she heard the clicks
and saw light flicker off your lens.

Trust held you both and the moment
in the air, until I came up.
Maybe you looked back. The bird flew.

Low or High Tide

One or the other was always there
probing the long bill into the surf
or into salty foam when the waves went out.

Sea rivulets running in sand, cold feet,
angry squawks, the willet watched the wind
on the water, moved in and out of the light,
the spreading world at the tip of his bill.

The Preacher

My hand, the Preacher was saying, shaking
his head rather, his hand occupied. He stood
tall and tickled, three feet above the strand,
the tide coming back, Ohio as far

as sin from his thoughts. His pole
arced and dancing in the air,
his hand working the bale, letting line
out as it ran and reeling in fast and steady

as it slackened. Whatever he'd hooked,
in his mind he was recounting fish stories:
Jonah and the Whale; Jesus by the Sea of Galilee;
in Peter's boat—the net almost breaking with 153

fish. Two feet back of his right shoulder,
the Preacher's thin spouse stood, iPhone
raised, thumb poised above the button,
her face already beaming the smile.

In her mind she was recording his triumph.
A small crowd gathered behind them waited.
Don't let loose of the drag, said the barefoot
local on his left. *My hand and arm tingle*

the Preacher was saying. *Keep the line
tight, tight*! said the local. *She's in the trough
in front of us. If you're going to lose her,
this is where you'll lose her. Let her run,*

Larry, he said, *but don't slack the line.*
The Preacher had begun walking west,
chasing the pull. Maybe the Shepherd
was yanking him now. *Even if I have*

to lose it, he was saying prayer-like,
more to himself than to us,
I would love to see what I've snagged.
The tail, said the local. *See the tail?*

Larry. He pointed to the closest wave.
It's a ray! A ray. About a three-four-
footer. It's a ray all right, he said,
as we all saw the line go dead.

Winter in the Marsh I

I saw a fiddler crab,
my first of the season.
Dark clouds
had cleared—a warm,
summery day in mid-January.

More cold would come.
The fiddler crab was still dark shelled,
a soft-green tint was on the large claw,
and a green was on the bottoms of the spike-rush.
There was time. My love was near.

Winter in the Marsh II

Then the edges of the trails were open.
You could see deep into the woods,
as into deep space.

Walking behind you,
I sometimes thought I knew you well,
how you'd look down at the gravel path,
trying to find your way across our years.

Always my Italian mother's closed door.

Even when I looked up and found you
staring at me
as if my soul lay between us
on the kitchen table.

How I loved walking behind you in the winter marsh,
calling out, *A great egret! A blue heron landing!*
making you smile as I knew how to,

holding you so tight there was no space between us.

Where the Croatan Touches the Marsh

On the coldest day
we walked as the sun crested the forest
and lightened new leaves and greened grasses
under sparkles of hoar frost
that had turned railings white overnight.

It lay thick and slicked boardwalks and bridges.
A skin of ice on shallow ponds
breathed a quiet over everything
and paused us
above a sleeping world.

The only walkers,
we moved closer. Maybe the light
that came over sleeping greens
warmed us too. Across the bay
Swansboro grew bright in the light.

When the Tide Was Out

When the tide was out,
I followed barefoot in your footprints
and felt the sea that filled your prints,
and the weight and warmth of you

warm the soles of my feet and rise
up my shins, tingling the back
of my knees, my thighs, my backside,
coursing my neck and down again.

Suddenly I was in your embrace
so close and tight, we were one.
And the sound of the sea,
the warmth of the sea air filled me.

Late January, 2020

When the wind was down,
warblers everywhere you looked.
Robins and cardinals
called from the woods.
Marsh rush grass had greened
to the tips. I caught us
walking with a forward lean.

Frost

That morning I followed.
I couldn't or wouldn't shake the chill.
The gap between us widened.

The slick frost on some boardwalks
maybe made the walking tenuous, too.
It didn't matter. Frost crystals
had settled. The remark had left
scaly impressions, and I was
rivet tight. Damp, greening air

would have filled us as we walked.
At the boat landing dock, you turned.
I was yours again.

The Last Walker

Wind made the sea choppy and squeezed
a sandy foam out of its belly and across the shore.
The few walkers hunched discouraged and left.

What ring-billed gulls had come
sat low, holding themselves stone tight.

A willet stood
dipping his long bill in the retreating tide
and rubbing it across his chest.

The fog closed the door. The wind picked up.
The birds and I moved inland.

Behind us, wind swallowed the faint sounds of the sea.

Canopy of Trees

Look down, you tell yourself.
Look out. Let it go.
Let the dark clouds stay in the distance.

The training exercises. The rumble
of artillery. Thundering bangs
below a far, dark horizon.
A chopper's blades coming nearer.
The cold edge on the wind.

The canopy of trees blunts.

Three great egrets land not far
and wait the tide and fish coming
in. The dark water below the bridge
comforts our eyes. A wave of sun
stretches clouds. Two egrets land

in a far, green tree. They face us.
A great blue heron comes in,
stands tall, watches everything.

Two Willets

That day the tide was out so far
the salt flats were dry,
and the ocean pulled at the marsh.
Even at our thoughts.
We'd been together so long,
I couldn't remember from when.
All the rivulets ran toward Dubling Creek
and out to sea. But two willets
probed across a damp salt flat pond,
and we two close together watched them.

Easy to Love

Even driving you from Cedar Point
up the Emerald Isle Bridge arching the sound
and toward the Crystal Coast and Bogue Banks,

it's easy to love how you look out. Your face beams
at one white egret along the hummocks and small islands
of green. I hear it in your voice, though I glance

quick—bridge railings are so perilously low.
Paradise gladdens your morning.
Seeing any large bird sets your day like a map.

Homecoming

Yesterday a fiddler crab crawled along
the dry mud path of an inlet off Dubling Creek
and one stirred at the rim of a mud hole

but didn't come out. Though the tide was far
and the sun warm, a breeze from the northwest

had a chill touch. Today, two crawled along the same inlet
mud path and scuttled into the greening warming grass
before we could fully see them. Still, fiddlers are coming

back to the salt marsh. In the sun, the mid-day grows warm.
I follow you, reappraise all your best angles, and smile.

The Neighbor's Holly

You could see the red clusters,
robins going in,
four, five, six at a time,
fluttering above the berries,
tree branches shaking.

It was late February, a great wind,
cold rain against windows.
The yards littered with robins,
plump robins
we'd loved all our lives

were filling up for a journey.
Maybe they'd dallied
like us talking a little too long.
Now a looming storm
and unknown winds hounded them.

When the Heron Paced

Usually he walked the western edge,
watching the surface of the pond
for a glint of silver,

but that day he paced inside
the black wrought iron fence enclosure.
The neighbors gone, the backyard empty,

except for their dog who threw a bark
or three from the balcony.
We all could claim years of watching

freshwater lakes, ponds, and maybe
a marsh but never of seeing a great blue
pacing, so. If suddenly this bird grew

unnerved about the journey north, why
not leave to younger ones the travel
rush, the yards and fences and barking dogs

we've made? He did stand a long time
at the far left, looking over the fence
and pond before turning and flying off.

When Spring Came

Who was watching
that day when fog cocooned us
in the marsh?

We became a whisper
and along the tide trails
found tender greens in the lowest places,
in new leaves of the bracken
rising out of coffee-colored marsh springs,
in cedars that hung over us heavy with dew.

And the trumpet vines
at eye-level above a boardwalk surprised us,
their yellow flowers fragrant, as a lost paradise,
already spilling themselves totally over the world.

The Pull

A wooden pathway
winds over a bog. Some
strangled and sprawled cedars
like an armful of kindling
lie leaching heavy
odors into dark muck.

Seething fumes encircle us.

When the tide comes back,
you can taste a green growth
rising skyward,
pulling your step and mine.

Ash Wednesday Night

and Saturday
under a black and red-orange sky,
peepers peeping ...
deliciously peeping all our spring hungers.

And then that next Monday
in a chilly morning along the sea
a black skimmer—
red bill with a black tip,
black cap, black wings, white chest, red legs—
a black skimmer standing.

On the Boat Landing Dock

So, we stood.
Mullets were jumping.
We wondered aloud. Maybe a soft moan.
We hadn't seen an osprey that year.

And then out of the west,
out of the sky a large bird.
An osprey, you said. *It's an osprey*.

It came,
our wish,
and dove twice before us.
For itself, it dove there
where mullets had jumped.

I Was the Salt Marsh

I was the salt marsh,
you were the sea—
the waters flowing in, flowing out.

I was the sand and mud
that drank and drank my fill

and oozed silt
heavy with pollens and seeds
and leaf-muck to the sea.

Morning Concert

All night the peepers must have gathered,
all the neighborhood tree frogs
must have come down from the trees
and gathered at our little pond.

In the dark we could hear something
was up outdoors, a vibration
through our windows and doors,
sound gathering and rising
from a thousand peepers

gathered and standing side by side
like blades of grass humming in the wind,
until we opened doors
and raised windows,

the sound bursting in,
filling our houses,
a river of song rushing in on us.
And we stood tense in our days of fears,
listening as our ears and our mouths,

our clothes grew heavy with song.
Even our eyes filled and overflowed,
squeezing out sadness, our worries, and fears
until we couldn't help but let it all go.

Late March

I catch a glint of dark green
in a stalk of spartina along a trail
in the salt marsh and maybe another
and another greening ... Maybe.

Only in a day or three, I stop
amazed by the greening stalk
breaking out of the top of the old—
a garter shedding its dry, dead husk.

The Willets' Way

Winters we found the willets
in gray plumage, long legs and straight bills,
mostly alone, fishing along the surf.

Some say their eyes are good day and night.
Ours were too, once, but we are lucky
to be travelling still together.

That April day when we found the two
in the salt marsh, they wore their spiffy
mottled brown. We were packing

for the long trek back to summer
in Wisconsin. Exiting was finding them
together having taken charge

of the salt marsh for their nesting time.
They have such a deliberate walk. They
pause like robins before probing.

Amazing is how they share chores.
There is an art in learning to live together
in a place and in how to take leave of it.

Dubling Creek

The gibbous moon was in its waxing phase.
The tides were high,
and Dubling Creek took all the water
and carried it in its wide apron to the White Oak River,
to the sea. I'd seen young women in the mountain
village of Ruota carry pinecones, kindling,
and animal bedding in wide aprons
or in outer skirts pulled up,
the bundles tight against their chest.

And so, Dubling Creek's lap swelled,
the high tides in its lap
until it lay the water down
and out over the salt marsh,
and the salt marsh drank its fill.

Even the farthest shadowed crevices drank.
The air above the marsh sang with morning birds.
All the dry hummocks in the bay greened,
and the grasses greened along the edges
of the bay and greened along the inlet banks.
Then the great snowy egrets came to fish.
A great blue heron landed,
and I followed on your heels thinking
of all the women laying their bundles down.

All That Spring

Walking behind you
I'd come to know
the back of you—
how your sides curved
in, to small hips,
how your tush
held itself as you walked
on shapely legs narrowing
to sculpted ankles
thin and fine as violet stems.

I imagined
thumbs and index fingers
rubbing along them
as I inhaled
the light and dark of the petals.

Two Looking at Two

> *"... earth in one unlooked-for favor"*
> Robert Frost

A pair of ospreys built a new nest
on a sheared-off top of a dead pine
over a trail. We heard their loud calls
from far across an estuary,
rainwater trickling out of the woods,
and saw the one circle and come down
on her. She screeched and screeched out,
and he rose up and went out over the trees,
and we circled the wet marshland.
When we passed under their tree and looked up,
we two saw them sitting shoulder to shoulder
on the pile of sticks and looking down at us.
I thought they saw us two, shoulder to shoulder,
before they rose and made a wide circle
over the tide-full salt marsh.

When You Stopped

Remember when you stopped
to look at great egrets
out along Dubling Creek
and I came up
and stood beside you
and draped an arm
across your shoulders
like that blue scarf
of Merino wool you
so love? Remember how
you then stepped back
and my arm slid
naturally down
to the small of your back?

We Met As in a Dream

Later that morning we walked the salt marsh
bundled up against a north wind
that gathered at the edges
and brushed through the pines
with its heavy broom. Five egrets

on the western side of Dubling Creek,
their backs against rush grass along the bank,
their heads tucked into hunched shoulders,
faced southeast, the sun
bright on the slits of their left eyes.

You stopped on a bridge over an estuary
to look at the high-tide-flooded marsh.
I thought of the few ice-encrusted grass tufts
in a rivulet deep in the woods. You turned, kissed
me, said, *Because you exist and I exist.*

Sunday Morning

Churches were closed because of the virus.
Over the salt marsh a breeze off the ocean.
The osprey was on her new nest. Close
by, he circled and came in, and you
loved how they greeted each other.

On a short bridge above an estuary you stopped.
Listened. You said, I would greet you too,
and brushed your lips across mine.
Warm already along the tide trails where
we passed a gentle person in pink. Her smile
a butterfly, she whispered, *Good morning*.

After Islander Beach Opened Again

An early May early morning,
we took the Coast Guard Road to the sea.
Except for a young woman
walking her dog, we were alone.

We walked southwest into a chill
wind, sun warm on our backs.

Pelicans, gulls, and sandpipers
had gathered on a sandbar off
a shallow cove of ocean with gentle
waves. More birds kept coming

slow and low into the chattering
morning, heating up in the morning sun.

How easy to let everything drop
and come in low onto a warm sandbar.
I turned and walked back to you
and your pile of large shells.

Since then, I've carried an ember
inside and outside stoked by the wind.

Acknowledgements

"Daughters" in review@roanoke.edu
"When the Tide Was Out," "When Spring Came," "Emerald Isle,"
"Then," and "You Pucker Your Mouth ..." in *Tideland News*

About the Author

Franco Pagnucci, Emeritus Professor of English, has published storytelling books, a chapbook, seven volumes of poetry, and two selected poetry anthologies.

His poems have won awards including the Edna Meudt Narrative Poetry Award. *Firstborn* - selected by WLA as Outstanding Work of Poetry, 2017.

Essays have appeared in publications such as *Christian Science Monitor* and *Commonweal*, his poetry is included in *News of the Universe*, *Best American Poetry 1999*, and *American Voices*. "The Death of an Elephant" podcast, *slowdownshow*, episode 192.

photo by Susan Pagnucci

Also Available from the Author

Again The Red Fox (Water's Edge Press, 2024)
Firstborn (North Star Press, 2016)
Breath of the Onion: Italian-American Anecdotes
    (North Star Press, 2015)
Tracks on Damp Sand (North Star Press, 2014)
Ancient Moves (Bur Oak Press, 1998)
I Never Had a Pet (Bur Oak Press, 1992)
Out Harmsen's Way (Fireweed Press, 1991)
New Roads Old Towns (A Rountree Publication,
    UW-Platteville, 1988)
Face the Poem (Bur Oak Press, 1979)

www.ingramcontent.com/pod-product-compliance
Lightning Source LLC
Chambersburg PA
CBHW030529080526
44586CB00011B/378